BEFORE WE WERE FREE

by
Julia Alvarez

Teacher Guide

Written by
Veda Boyd Jones

Edited by
Nancy Snow Smith

Note

The Borzoi Book hardcover edition of the book, published by Alfred A. Knopf, ©2002, was used to prepare this guide. The page references may differ in other editions.

Please note: This novel deals with sensitive, mature issues. Parts may contain profanity, sexual references, and/or descriptions of violence. Please assess the appropriateness of this book for the age level and maturity of your students prior to reading and discussing it with them.

ISBN 1-58130-827-2

Copyright infringement is a violation of Federal Law.

© 2004 by Novel Units, Inc., Bulverde, Texas. All rights reserved. No part of this publication may be reproduced, translated, stored in a retrieval system, or transmitted in an~~~~~~~~~ ~~~~~~~ (~~~~~~~~~ ~~~~~~~~~ photocopying, recording, or otherwise) without prior written per~~~~~~

Photocopying of student worksheets by a classroom teacher at a ~~~~~~~ for his/her own class is permissible. Reproduction of any part of ~~~~ system, by for-profit institutions and tutoring centers, or for com~~~~~

Novel Units is a registered trademark of Novel Units, Inc.

Printed in the United States of America.

To order, contact your local school
supply store, or—

Table of Contents

Skills and Strategies

Thinking
 Interpreting evidence,
 compare/contrast, forming
 opinions, identifying
 stereotypes, paradox,
 pros/cons, research

Comprehension
 Cause/effect, classifying,
 details, generalizing,
 inferencing, main idea,
 predicting, summarizing

Writing
 Article, description, list,
 poem, narrative, letter,
 report, editorial

Listening/Speaking
 Discussion, interview, oral
 report, role-playing

Vocabulary
 Compound words,
 context clues

Literary Elements
 Analogy, characterization,
 descriptions, foreshadowing,
 plot development, setting,
 point of view, simile, theme

Across the Curriculum
 Art—architecture, drawing;
 Science—agriculture,
 weather, botany; Social
 Studies—maps, culture,
 history, politics, laws;
 Math—survey statistics

Genre: young adult fiction

Setting: The novel begins in 1960 in the Dominican Republic under the dictatorship of General Rafael Molino Trujillo. The final chapters are set in New York City.

Point of View: first-person, from twelve-year-old Anita de la Torre's viewpoint

Themes: coming of age, accepting change, dealing with terror and grief, political unrest, freedom, hope

Conflict: person vs. person, person vs. society, person vs. self

Style: narrative

Date of First Publication: 2002

Summary

Anita de la Torre turns twelve during the Trujillo totalitarian regime in the Dominican Republic. Many of her family members have already fled the country for the United States, but Anita's father and uncle remain to lead the resistance in a coup. Anita is protected from many aspects of the planned overthrow, but she soon learns that her father plans to kill the dictator and that her family is in danger. During this time, she becomes a señorita (woman) when she has her first menstrual period, and develops feelings for Sam, the son of the American consul.

After General Trujillo is assassinated, everything falls apart for the conspirators. Anita's father and uncle are taken to prison, and Anita and her mother hide in a house next to the Italian embassy for over a month. Anita and her mother are secretly flown out of the country to join family members in New York City. Anita vows to return to her country, but when the family learns of her father's execution, they decide to stay in the United States where they can be free.

Teacher Note

This novel addresses sensitive issues such as suicide, a young girl's first menstrual cycle, political dissent, assassination, death of a parent, rape, and torture. It also provides a forum to discuss resiliance, hope, freedom, courage, and religion. Please consider your class and community before discussing these themes.

About the Author

Julia Alvarez was born in New York City on March 27, 1950. Her parents took her to their homeland, the Dominican Republic, when she was an infant. Her father became involved in the insurgent movement against the dictator, and he and his family escaped from the island shortly before he was to be arrested. At age ten, Alvarez returned to New York City. As a young girl who had learned limited English by attending American school in the Dominican Republic, she was frustrated in a city where English was spoken as a first language. She turned to books, learned the language, and lost herself in stories. By high school she knew that she wanted to be a writer, but it was not until much later that she realized there was a publication market for her personal experiences, bridging the cultural gap between the Dominican Republic and the United States.

Alvarez graduated from Middlebury College and earned a master's degree in creative writing from Syracuse University. She has taught writing, and her poetry and fiction have won many awards. She is currently a writer-in-residence at Middlebury College.

Before We Were Free is her first book for young people. It was selected as one of the best books of the year by the *Miami Herald* in 2002 and was named an ALA Notable and an ALA Best Book for Young Adults in 2003. It was selected to receive the 2002 Americas Award for Children's and Young Adult Literature, sponsored by the national Consortium of Latin American Studies Programs. Alvarez lives with her husband in Vermont. Her official Web site (live at the printing of this guide) is **www.alvarezjulia.com.**

Major Characters

Anita de la Torre: twelve-year-old narrator who attends the American school in the Dominican Republic

Mami: Anita's mother, Carmen

Papi: Anita's father, Mundo; a leader in the plot to assassinate the dictator

Sam (Sammy) Washburn: son of the American consul; Anita's first love

Oscar Mancini: son of a man who works at the Italian embassy; Anita's second love

El Jefe: the dictator, General Rafael Molino Trujillo

Chucha: long-time family servant from Haiti

Lucinda: Anita's older sister

Mundín: Anita's older brother

Carla: Anita's cousin who escapes to New York City

Lorena: maid who is suspected of being a spy for the secret police

Tío Toni: Anita's uncle who is involved in the plot to overthrow General Trujillo

Initiating Activities

Choose one or more of the following activities to introduce the novel.
1. Multi-media: Show videotapes, pictures, and photographs of the Dominican Republic. Provide several books about the Dominican Republic to use as resources throughout the study of the novel. Also include articles, books, and pictures of New York City. Allow each student to look at one resource material for three minutes before passing it to the next person. Continue passing resources until students have seen most of them.

2. Geography/Culture: Show maps of the Dominican Republic and New York City. Give vital statistics about the Dominican Republic, its population, cultural diversity, major industries, and the history of the overthrow of General Trujillo. Show the flag of the Dominican Republic.

3. Social Studies: Have students research how the diplomatic service works and explain the difference between an ambassador and a consul.

4. Social Studies: Have students research how an embargo works and the impact one has on a small island nation.

5. Social Studies/Math: Have students research the types of governments found in the Caribbean Islands and Central America, create a chart indicating the type of government, and determine the percentages of democracies and dictatorships.

6. Social Issues: Conduct an opinion poll on whether or not peaceful protests are effective. Students can research peaceful protests in their local newspapers for examples.

7. Predicting: Give students the following clues and have them write a paragraph predicting what they think will happen in the story: dictator, embassy, family compound, first love, secret police, diary, arrest, asylum, hiding.

Vocabulary Activities

1. Vocabulary Sort: Have students sort vocabulary words into categories (e.g., nouns, verbs, adjectives, and adverbs). See the graphic organizer on page 7 of this guide.

2. Sentences: Have students select three or four vocabulary words and use them in one sentence. They may do this with the vocabulary lists for each chapter.

3. Word Maps: Have students complete word maps for vocabulary words (see below). For example: nuclear (9), embargo (28), censors (40), cadavers (49), potential (56), interference (69), chauffeur (87), khaki (91), profiles (105), tragedy (113), terminal (143), and stressed (157).

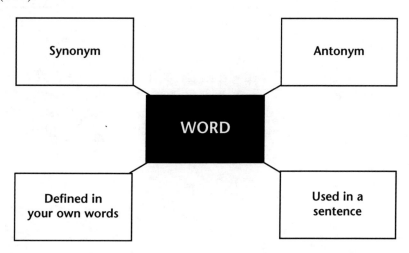

4. Context Clues: Remind students of the various types of context clues such as description, example, synonym, contrast, and comparison. Examples of words from the novel to practice using context clue strategies include: vile (19), contradict (23), bewitched (36), potential (56), sentimental (72), hypnotizing (80), vacate (95), accommodations (114), ambush (150), and cronies (151).

5. Prefix Hints: Have students identify the target vocabulary words with prefixes and categorize them. For example: inter—intervention (43) and interference (69); re—reaction (8) and revised (95); dis—disarray (70) and dissidents (82).

6. Vocabulary Charades: Have students act out some of the vocabulary words that refer to actions and have other students guess which ones they are. For example: bawling (8), traipse (15), preoccupied (32), squeamish (66), hypnotizing (80), brandishing (98), and ransacks (104).

7. Specific Categories: Have students list vocabulary words related to specific categories. For example: Political Terms—consul (6), embargo (28), inauguration (43), immunity (44), amnesty (47), assassinate (75), dissidents (82), exiles (85), and liberate (85).

8. Visual Images: Have students use an encyclopedia, the Internet, or other resources to find pictures of vocabulary words. For example: jalousies (15), compound (22), crèche (39), foliage (41), buffet (64), chauffeur (87), khaki (91), monogram (106), and terminal (143).

9. Word Map—Verb: Have students complete word maps for the vocabulary verbs (see below). For example: economize (11), contradict (23), bewitched (36), pardoned (59), persists (86), and ruptured (123).

Word Map for a Verb

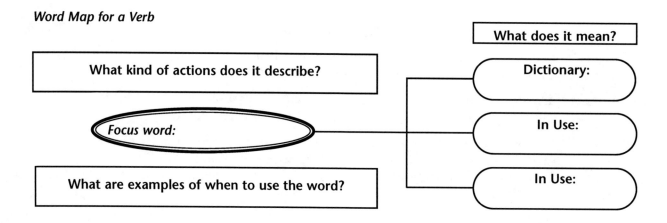

10. Sentences: Have students choose words from the vocabulary lists and write a sentence about a main character using each word. Then write a sentence about themselves using the same words. For example: vigorously (20), tension (32), grievances (55), sentimental (72), glamorous (79), animated (84), languid (94), privacy (108), and sophisticated (156).

Vocabulary Sort

Noun	Verb	Adjective	Adverb

Using Predictions

We all make predictions as we read—little guesses about what will happen next, how a conflict will be resolved, which details will be important to the plot, which details will help fill in our sense of a character. Students should be encouraged to predict, to make sensible guesses as they read the novel.

As students work on their predictions, these discussion questions can be used to guide them: What are some of the ways to predict? What is the process of a sophisticated reader's thinking and predicting? What clues does an author give to help us make predictions? Why are some predictions more likely to be accurate than others?

Create a chart for recording predictions. This could be either an individual or class activity. As each subsequent chapter is discussed, students can review and correct their previous predictions about plot and characters as necessary.

Use the facts and ideas the author gives.

Use your own prior knowledge.

Apply any new information (i.e., from class discussion) that may cause you to change your mind.

Predictions

_____

_____

_____

_____

Prediction Chart

What characters have we met so far?	What is the conflict in the story?	What are your predictions?	Why did you make these predictions?

Character Analysis

Directions: Working in small groups, discuss the attributes of the characters listed below. In each character's box, write several words or phrases that describe him or her.

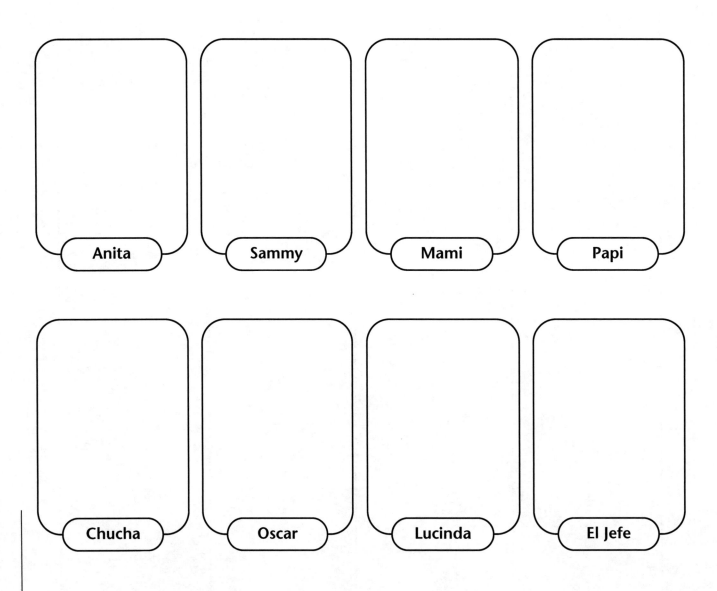

Anita

Sammy

Mami

Papi

Chucha

Oscar

Lucinda

El Jefe

Graphing Plot Lines

Characters

Setting

Problem

Climax

Resolution

Beginning

Building Action

Metaphors and Similes

A **metaphor** is a comparison between two unlike objects. For example, "he was a human tree." A **simile** is a comparison between two unlike objects that uses the words *like* or *as*. For example, "the color of her eyes was like the cloudless sky."

Directions: Complete the chart below by listing metaphors and similes from the novel, as well as the page numbers on which they are found. Identify metaphors with an "M" and similes with an "S." Translate the comparisons in your own words, and then list the objects being compared.

Metaphors/Similes	Ideas/Objects Being Compared
1. Translation:	
2. Translation:	
3. Translation:	

Foreshadowing Chart

Foreshadowing is the literary technique of giving clues to coming events in a story.

Directions: What examples of foreshadowing do you recall from the story? If necessary, skim through the chapters to find examples of foreshadowing. List at least four examples below. Explain what clues are given, then list the coming event that is suggested.

Foreshadowing	Page #	Clues	Coming Event

Chapter One, pp. 1–12

Anita is in class on November 11, 1960, when her aunt and the principal come to the classroom door. Anita's cousin, Carla García, is told to pack all her school belongings, and Anita rides with her cousin back to the family compound. The García sisters are told their father waits for them at the airport. They each change their clothes, pick one special item to bring, and leave with their mother and an American consul. Anita helps her old nanny, Chucha, move into their house. Eccentric Chucha sleeps in a coffin and always wears purple. She claims to foresee the future and tells Anita that she will see her cousins before they come back and after Anita is free. At supper, a black butterfly, a sign of impending death, flaps into the dining room. That evening Anita goes through Carla's school supplies but decides she's too sad to use them. She puts them in Carla's backpack, but later discovers the odd-shaped eraser on her bed.

Vocabulary
tic (3)
benefactor (4)
consul (6)
reaction (8)
bawling (8)
strewn (9)
nuclear (9)
straggly (9)
economize (11)
recitation (12)

Discussion Questions

1. Why does Mrs. Brown give the "not-so-good" parts in the skits to the Dominicans? What does this say about her character? *(Mrs. Brown teaches at the American school and favors the American students. She may be American herself. She may be biased against the Dominican children. Answers will vary. p. 1)*

2. The author cleverly works in the date when the story begins. How does she do this? What day is it? *(The author describes the class clown's activities. The day before the story begins, he writes "No homework tonight" above the date, November 10, 1960. Therefore, the story starts on November 11, 1960. p. 2)*

3. The author uses present tense to tell the story. Why? Is this effective? *(She can make the action seem more immediate. Answers will vary.)*

4. Anita is confused because she is not asked to pack her school belongings at the same time as her cousin Carla. What does this say about Anita's family ties? *(Anita's extended family is very close. pp. 3, 9)*

5. Anita helps Carla pick the jewelry box to take to the United States. She reasons that choosing it allows Carla to take more than one thing. What does this say about Anita's personality? *(Answers will vary. p. 7)*

6. Anita doesn't know if she can believe her mother when she says that they will see the cousins soon. Why? What does this say about Anita's character and her mother's character? *(Anita's mother tells Anita's grandmother that her son is fine even though they haven't seen him in months. Anita thinks her mother may just be trying to make her cousins feel better. Answers will vary. pp. 8–9)*

7. **Prediction:** What do you think Chucha means when she says, "You will see them before they come back but only after you are free,"on page 11 of the novel?

8. **Prediction:** Whose death do you think the black butterfly foreshadows?

Supplementary Activities

1. Literary Analysis/Symbols: The snow globe can be seen as a symbol of the new life the Garcías will experience in the United States. Have the students begin a list of symbols that occur in the book.

2. Literary Analysis/Predictions: Using the Prediciton Chart on page 9 of this guide, have students fill in the chart as they read the novel.

3. Literary Analysis/Characterization: Have students begin their Character Analysis charts (see page 10 of this guide).

4. Literary Analysis/Plot Development: Have students begin their Graphing Plot Lines charts (see page 11 of this guide) to use as they read this story.

5. Social Studies: Anita says people do things differently in Haiti. Have students locate the Dominican Republic and Haiti on a map. Have students research three ways the cultures are different.

6. Literary Elements: **Similes**—The author uses similes such as Oscar's hand "...waving and dipping like a palm tree in a cyclone" (p. 3). Using the Metaphors and Similes chart on page 12 of this guide, have students begin a list of similes and add to the list as they read.

Chapter Two, pp. 13–25

The day after the Garcías leave, men in black Volkswagens surround the compound and search it. Anita is told they are SIM, the secret police. That night the entire family sleeps on mattresses on the floor. While the secret police stake out the compound, Anita stays home from school. Everyone whispers because they fear their conversations are being recorded. Anita learns that Tío Toni was involved in a plot to overthrow the dictator. The American consul and his family move into one of the empty houses in the compound. Anita befriends Sammy, the consul's son, who is her age. They explore the compound and discover that someone is in Tío Toni's house. Because they fear their parents will forbid them to explore, they don't reveal their discovery.

Vocabulary
jalousies (15)
askew (15)
traipse (15)
colicky (17)
vile (19)
custody (20)
vigorously (20)
proposition (21)
compound (22)
contradict (23)

Discussion Questions

1. Anita left her baby doll pajamas lying on the floor that morning. What do you think her room looks like? Why? *(It is probably messy because she's used to having a housekeeper pick up after her. Answers will vary. p. 14)*

2. Why does Anita cling to her mother while the search continues? What does this say about her character? *(She is afraid the men will harm her mother. Answers will vary. p. 15)*

3. Why does the family sleep on mattresses on the floor? *(The parents want them all low so that bullets aimed higher won't hit them. p. 17)*

4. Mami tells Anita to stop asking questions because she doesn't have answers. Why doesn't Mami tell Anita what she knows? *(Anita is known to talk too much. Answers will vary. pp. 17–18)*

5. Why doesn't Anita realize earlier that her family doesn't like the dictator? What does this say about Anita's character? *(Answers will vary. Anita never questions that the pictures hanging in the school and in their home must be there. Anita is very trusting. p. 20)*

6. Anita doesn't contradict Sam when he says he lives in the best country in the world, although previous to learning about the dictator she believed she lived in the best country. What does this say about her character? *(She did not question her government before the secret police came, and she was happy in her country. p. 23)*

7. Why don't Sammy and Anita tell their parents about the person in Tío Toni's house? *(They don't want to be denied access to parts of the compound. Answers will vary. p. 25)*

8. **Prediction:** Who is in Tío Toni's house?

Supplementary Activities

1. Literary Elements: **Similes**—Have students add similes to their list. Point out Mami letting the secret police enter the house "...like the toilet is overflowing and these are the plumbers..." (p. 14)

2. Research: Have students research the television show "Howdy Doody."

3. Writing: Have students pretend they are Anita and write a letter to Carla explaining how she feels about not going to school and having the secret police around the compound.

Chapter Three, pp. 26–41

Anita's mother warns her not to talk with her friends about what is happening at home. Anita's tendency to talk too much earned her the nickname of "Little Parrot." She goes back to school where Sam is the new student in her class. Anita is warned against talking freely in front of the new maid. At school the Secret Santa game is cancelled because the Dominican parents think there is too much tension and too many secrets caused by the embargo. Anita overhears her father talking in code on the phone, and she wonders what it is all about. The family prepares for Christmas by purchasing special foods, even though the construction company is not doing well, and they are watching their budget. On Christmas Eve, Anita sees lights in her uncle's cabin.

Vocabulary
apprehensive (27)
embargo (28)
tension (32)
preoccupied (32)
bewitched (36)
nutrition (38)
crèche (39)
censors (40)
foliage (41)

Discussion Questions

1. Is it wise of Mami not to tell Anita too much? *(It is probably wise because Anita might accidentally repeat information that could put a friend or family member in danger. p. 28)*

2. Mami tells Anita to watch what she says in front of the new maid. Why? *(They don't know the maid's background, and she could be a spy. With the murder of their friends, they are being very careful. p. 29)*

3. Mrs. Brown won't answer the question about how the Dominican Republic has warranted an embargo. Why? *(She is afraid to say anything against the country's leaders. Answers will vary. p. 34)*

4. Why doesn't Anita want Sam at her birthday celebration? What does this say about her character? *(She lied and told him she was already twelve, and she doesn't want him to know she lied. Answers will vary. p. 36)*

5. What does Papi say is the key to improving the lives of their countrymen? Do you agree? *(Education is the key that will help all children rise to their potential. Answers will vary. p. 37)*

6. Anita is insulted when she's asked what Santa will bring her. Why? Would you be insulted? *(She no longer believes in Santa Claus and thinks Mrs. Washburn believes she is much younger than she is because she's small. Answers will vary. p. 40)*

7. **Prediction:** Where is Chucha going with the canned food?

Supplementary Activities

1. Research: Have students research embargos the United States has joined. Have some students present oral reports on their findings.

2. Research: Have students research Christmas traditions in the Dominican Republic.

3. Art: Have students draw a sea grape tree as described on page 34 of the novel.

4. Writing: Have students write a poem about a gift-giving tradition.

Chapter Four, pp. 42–53

Writing her thoughts in her diary helps Anita think things through. She has a big crush on Sammy, but when she writes something about him, she erases it so no one will read it. School is delayed because many Americans are going home for President Kennedy's inauguration. When Oscar visits the compound, he explains how the dictator controls the country with violence. Sammy sees someone in Tío Toni's cabin, but Chucha tells Anita to tell Sammy that it is "someone he did not see." Mami asks Anita not to go to that end of the compound and not to write in her diary until they are free.

Vocabulary
supervision (42)
inauguration (43)
intervention (43)
immunity (44)
amnesia (47)
amnesty (47)
crucify (48)
cadavers (49)
banish (51)

Discussion Questions

1. Compare and contrast the presidential elections held in the United States with those held in the Dominican Republic. Which system do you want to live under? *(Contrast U.S. democracy with presidential elections every four years and two-term limits with Trujillo's election in which only his name is on the ballot. Answers will vary. p. 44)*

2. Why does Anita feel she is a hand-me-down human being? Do you think that her mental and spiritual sides are also hand-me-down? Defend your answer. *(She attributes her physical characteristics to her various relatives. Answers will vary. p. 45)*

3. Why doesn't Anita want Oscar at the compound, and why is she hurt when she finds Sammy and Oscar playing? *(She is worried that the boys will be enemies and then feels confused about them being friends without her. Answers will vary. pp. 46–47)*

4. Why does Chucha tell Sammy that Toni is "someone he did not see"? *(She doesn't want the children to know information that could get anyone at the compound into trouble. Answers will vary. p. 50)*

5. Mami says, "But sometimes life without freedom is no life at all," and she says they must stay in the Dominican Republic. How does this apply to Anita's family? Do you agree with this statement? Why or why not? *(Someone must stay and fight for the citizens' rights instead of fleeing. Answers will vary. p. 52)*

6. **Prediction:** Will anyone read Anita's diary? Why or why not?

Supplementary Activities

1. Literary Elements/Foreshadowing: Introduce the concept of foreshadowing. Recall that Anita sees someone in Tío Toni's cabin whom the reader later finds out is Toni. Instruct students to keep a list of other examples of foreshadowing (see page 13 of this guide).

2. Writing: Have students write a list of freedoms they enjoy and compare the ways in which their freedoms differ from Anita's. Have students read their lists aloud.

3. Social Issues: Discuss how parents influence children. Ask students to list ways they are similar to their parents and ways they are different. Have them list both physical and behavioral traits.

4. Literary Analysis/Symbols: Have students add to their list of symbols. Mention that keeping a diary is a symbol of freedom of speech.

Chapter Five, pp. 54–64

Anita is told that Mr. Smith is a powerful man who likes pretty girls and takes the ones he wants. Therefore, parents are very careful about letting their daughters go to public places. The Washburns decide to hold Susie's fifteenth birthday party at the compound. Tío Toni is now out of hiding in the compound, and sometimes his friends drop in and talk for hours. He won't come to the party because he thinks he should lay low. While the new maid is out, Anita's house is swept for hidden microphones, but none are found. The maid is under suspicion because she was caught cleaning Papi's desk drawers. The night of the party, a band of secret police come, and Anita runs to Tío Toni's cabin to warn her father. Later at the party, El Jefe walks in.

Vocabulary
grievances (55)
potential (56)
pardoned (59)
buffet (64)

Discussion Questions

1. Do you think the family is unnecessarily concerned about their home being bugged and their maid being a spy? *(Answers will vary. pp. 58–60)*

2. How would you feel if someone listened in on your phone conversations or read your diary? *(Answers will vary.)*

3. Anita has wanted to be like Joan of Arc. Do you think Anita is a heroine? Why or why not? *(Answers will vary. p. 63)*

4. **Prediction:** Do you think Lorena is a spy? Why or why not?

Supplementary Activities

1. Social Studies: Have students research the custom of having quinceañera parties in the Dominican Republic.

2. Writing: Have students write a paragraph on the meaning of Chucha's folk saying, "The shrimp who falls asleep is carried off by the current" (p. 61).

Chapter Six, pp. 65–76

Papi and Mami are stunned when El Jefe makes an appearance at the party. They fear that their family is in danger because of Tío Toni's secret meetings. They also suspect the maid, Lorena, is a spy for the secret police. They must think of a plan to get rid of her, but first a bigger problem arises. El Jefe sends flowers to Lucinda. Because he is known to make young girls his mistresses, they must get Lucinda out of the country. The consul first thinks she can be a maid in America, but later decides she will accompany Susie to visit Susie's grandparents in Washington, D.C. During Lucinda's last night, Anita sleeps in her bed, and they confide secrets. That night Anita starts her first menstrual cycle. Lucinda helps and reassures her, but Anita doesn't want anyone else to know. Anita takes the soiled sheets to Chucha, who drapes them on the coffin and moves it to Lorena's room. Lorena screams when she sees the coffin and bloody sheets and packs to leave the compound.

Vocabulary
squeamish (66)
contaminated (67)
interference (69)
disarray (70)
consolation (71)
sentimental (72)
participating (75)
assassinate (75)

Discussion Questions

1. Why can't Mami simply fire the maid? *(She is afraid Lorena will go to the secret police and tell them all that she's observed at the compound. Answers will vary. pp. 65–66)*

2. The women hint at El Jefe's character when it comes to young girls. Is there a justifiable reason for Lucinda to become so upset? *(El Jefe is known to make young girls his mistresses. Answers will vary. pp. 67–69)*

3. Life is falling apart around Anita. Her cousins are gone, her sister is leaving, and the boys have been drinking and throwing up. She wants to be like Joan of Arc, cut her hair, and dress like a boy to be safe. Then another complication besets her. She starts her first menstrual period. Why doesn't she want her mother to know? Does this fit Anita's character? Why or why not? *(Her mother would worry more because she has another daughter who is now a señorita. Answers will vary. pp. 71–73)*

4. Anita feels, "It's *so* unfair to have to live in a country where you have to do stuff you feel bad about in order to save your life." Have students discuss what this means to them. *(Answers will vary. p. 75)*

5. **Prediction:** Chucha's dream does not include Papi flying away. What will happen to Papi?

Supplementary Activities

1. Social Studies/Culture: Have students make a list of superstitions that Lorena believes in and add other superstitions to the list.

2. Writing: Have students make a list of clothes they would take on a month-long visit to another country, keeping in mind that the airlines prefer travelers to take only two suitcases and one carry-on bag.

Chapter Seven, pp. 77–89

Anita must go to school on the day Lucinda leaves for the United States. She feels ill from her menstrual period and overwhelming sadness (compounded because the American school is closing) and goes home sick. At night when she lies in bed, she can hear the men talking outside her window. She becomes afraid, and her fear manifests itself in her inability to find words to express herself. She remains silent most of the time. One day Mr. Washburn drives the children to Oscar Mancini's home for private school. A traffic jam causes an accident, and the trunk of Mr. Washburn's car will not shut. A policeman sees guns in the trunk, but only asks Mr. Washburn to fix the trunk. They tie the trunk closed with a rope.

Vocabulary
collapse (77)
glamorous (79)
hypnotizing (80)
dissidents (82)
animated (84)
exiles (85)
liberate (85)
persists (86)
chauffeur (87)
wielding (88)

Discussion Questions

1. Anita starts putting her crucifix in her mouth when she needs extra good luck. What does this say about her character? *(She is religious and takes comfort in her spirituality. Answers will vary. p. 77)*

2. How does Sam feel about his sister leaving? Is this the same way Anita feels about her sister leaving? What do their reactions say about their characters? *(Sam is glad his bossy sister is leaving; Anita is sad. Their siblings are leaving the country for different reasons. Anita's sister is in danger, and Anita fears for her safety. pp. 77–78)*

3. Anita and her siblings react differently to the tension in their lives. Compare and contrast their reactions. *(Anita can't think of words to express herself; Lucinda breaks out in a rash; Mundín bites his nails. p. 80)*

4. Discuss Anita's plan to destroy her father's and uncle's suicide pills, yet save one for herself. What does this say about her state of mind? What other options might Anita have? *(Answers will vary. p. 82)*

5. Anita's crush on Sam has faded. Why? *(He hasn't lived up to her ideal of him, and the life and death situation has taken over in importance. Answers will vary. p. 87)*

6. **Prediction:** Oscar's father no longer comes to meetings so that his house can be a safe place if needed. Will Anita go to Oscar's house?

Supplementary Activities

1. Writing: Have students write a paragraph about a time when they were scared and how they overcame their fear.

2. Science: Have students find out how a short wave radio works.

3. Social Studies: Have students discover the part that radio can play in broadcasting information about alternative governments. Mention Radio Free Europe as an example.

4. Writing: Have students write an alternative ending to the encounter with the police in which the policemen confiscate the guns.

Chapter Eight, pp. 90–100

From the schoolroom at Oscar's house, the kids watch El Jefe walk from his mother's mansion. He is dressed in khakis, which is not his usual dress for a Tuesday. Oscar and Anita talk about being brave and afraid, and Oscar kisses Anita on the cheek. Her father comes for Anita and Mundín, and he appears to be in a hurry. The compound has many cars in it; the men have guns, and they drive off. When they return, they are triumphant until someone mentions that Pupo is missing. They leave to look for him. Mundín goes in a car to Oscar's house to check there. Mami calls and makes sure that the Mancinis keep him there.

Vocabulary
khaki (91)
languid (94)
deserted (95)
revised (95)
vacate (95)
brandishing (98)

Discussion Questions

1. Oscar understands the fear that Anita is living with. He says, "You can't be brave if you're not scared" (p. 93). What does this say about his character? How are his and Anita's feelings similar? *(Anita knows that Oscar is scared, too. Answers will vary. pp. 92–93)*

2. Papi turns to Anita in the car with an "if-looks-could-kill" look, but he quickly changes it. Why do you think he is so preoccupied, and how does Anita interpret his look? *(The last attempt on El Jefe failed because "Mr. Smith didn't show up at the picnic." Obviously tonight will be another attempt. Anita understands that her father does not mean the look for her. Answers will vary. p. 94)*

3. How does Anita know about the U.S. Constitution? *(She went to an American school and studied it there. pp. 95–96)*

4. When the men return, Papi says that they are free. What has happened? *(They have assassinated El Jefe. p. 98)*

5. Why doesn't Anita say goodbye to Papi when he leaves the second time? *(She is too frightened to talk. pp. 99–100)*

6. **Prediction:** Who is Pupo, and has he betrayed the men?

Supplementary Activities

1. Literary Elements: **Similes**—Have students add to their simile list. Remind them of the astronaut curled up "like an unborn baby" (p. 97) and Anita being unable to speak because the words are stuffed in her mouth "like a gag keeping me from talking" (p. 99).

2. Writing: Have students write a paragraph about a time when they did not bid someone goodbye and later wished they had.

Chapter Nine, pp. 101–107

Anita is terrified as she waits for the men to return. She vows to stay "one step ahead of being scared." She learns that Pupo is the head of the army. Finally she sleeps, but her dreams are mixed up. Chucha shakes her awake as the SIM rush in yelling "traitors" and ransack the room. The leader is nicknamed little Razor Blade. When El Jefe's body is found in the trunk of a Chevy in the garage, the SIM arrest Papi and Tío Toni. Mami makes calls, and Mr. Mancini comes over. He tells them to pack their bags quickly. Anita is paralyzed with fear, but Chucha throws some clothes and Anita's diary in a laundry bag for her. Chucha says, "It's time. Fly, fly free!"

Vocabulary
liberation (102)
denounce (102)
ransacks (104)
scouring (104)
profiles (105)
confiscated (105)
monogram (106)
paralysis (107)

Discussion Questions

1. Why does Anita change her plan to commit suicide? How does she hope to get away? *(She decides to take Papi and Chucha's advice: fly and be free.)*

2. How is Anita going to stay "one step ahead of being scared." *(She decides on an escape plan to the market through the back of the compound. p. 101)*

3. The official radio station does not announce El Jefe's death. Instead it plays organ music, which reminds Anita of an endless funeral. What does the music mean? *(It represents two funerals: the death of El Jefe and the death of the independence movement. Answers will vary. pp. 102–103)*

4. Why would Papi put El Jefe's body in his own garage, ignoring the possible risks it places on his family? *(Answers will vary. p. 104)*

5. Little Razor Blade tells Mami that they are taking Papi and Tío Toni "to the place where they took El Jefe." What does he mean? *(He means the SIM will kill them. Answers will vary. p. 104)*

6. **Prediction:** Will Chucha go with Mami and Anita to Mr. Mancini's home?

Supplementary Activity

1. Writing: Have students write a paragraph describing Anita's state of mind while she is in her room trying to pack.

Anita's Diary, pp. 108–137

Anita finds her diary among the clothes Chucha packed and writes about her life in hiding at the Mancinis' home. She and Mami hide in the walk-in closet. In case of a raid, their emergency plan is to hide in the crawl space in two small closets in the bathroom. They are smuggled food by the Mancinis (Tía Mari and Tío Pepe) who are the only ones in the household who know they are there. There are close calls. The SIM make a surprise visit and kill the Mancinis' two pet dogs when they are let outside. Oscar discovers Anita and her mother hiding in the closet, and he and Anita communicate by sending the queen of hearts card back and forth in books. Before Mundín is smuggled aboard a ship bound for America, he comes disguised as a girl to say goodbye to his mother and sister. In her diary, Anita writes about the freedom movement. Her last entry is written while hiding in the crawl space. After hearing a loud crash downstairs, she thinks the SIM are coming to take her away.

Vocabulary
privacy (108)
conspirators (109)
consequences (109)
procedure (110)
survivors (112)
tragedy (113)
accommodations (114)
incredible (120)
ruptured (123)
potential (127)

Discussion Questions

1. Tío Pepe tells Anita that she must think positively to survive tragedy. Do you think positive thinking can help a person survive? *(Answers will vary. p. 113)*

2. Tío Pepe says "boredom is a sign of the poverty of the mind." Do you agree with him? Why or why not? *(Answers will vary. p. 121)*

3. Compare and contrast the way Anita and her mother deal with their captivity. *(Anita writes in her diary to find peace. Her mother takes tranquilizers. Answers will vary. pp. 108–137)*

4. Why does Anita think she is in love with Oscar? Will this love fade like her love for Sam? Why or why not? *(Oscar seems to understand her feelings. Her second love is based on kindness, understanding, and friendship, and therefore may be more enduring. Answers will vary. pp. 126–136)*

5. Tío Pepe says that human beings aren't using their full potential. Do you agree? Why or why not? *(Answers will vary. pp. 127–128)*

6. Anita wonders if some people are so evil that nothing can change them. What do you think? *(Answers will vary. p. 128)*

7. Discuss how Mami and Papi were pulled into the revolutionary movement. Why did they stay to fight for freedom when so many of their family members left the country? *(Answers will vary. pp. 133–134)*

8. **Prediction:** Will the SIM capture Anita and Mami?

Supplementary Activities

1. Literary Analysis/Symbols: Have students add to their list of symbols used in the book.

2. Research: Have students find out what immunities are given to ambassadors and their families.

3. Writing: Have students make a list of books they would recommend for a twelve year old to read. Are any of the books Oscar picked on their lists?

4. Writing: Tío Pepe told Anita that famous prisoners found that if they kept a daily schedule, it helped them to handle the stress of imprisonment. Have students develop a schedule for themselves to follow on stressful school days.

Chapter Ten, pp. 138–151

Wimpy and the paratroopers rescue Anita and Mami and fly them out of the embassy grounds in a helicopter while the SIM are busy at a demonstration. Anita, her mother, sister, and brother are now living in New York City in her grandparent's rented hotel apartment. There is no news of Papi and Tío Toni, so the family settles to wait. Anita attends a Catholic school and writes her memories of her country. She also writes to Oscar, but mail service to the Dominican Republic has been suspended. Anita stops at a grocery store and fills up a cart, then starts to put things back. The manager stops her and takes her outside. She runs, afraid of deportation. Arriving at the apartment, she finds Mr. Washburn there. He has come to tell them that Papi and Tío Toni were executed.

Vocabulary
prediction (139)
temporary (141)
evacuation (141)
terminal (143)
deported (149)
ambush (150)
possibilities (150)
cronies (151)

Discussion Questions

1. Why is Anita horrified when she sees Anita Banana on TV? (*She refuses to think about staying in the United States instead of returning home. Answers will vary. p. 139*)

2. Why can't Anita go with her grandfather to get the medicine? What is the family's financial situation? (*The apartment rent will go up if the manager at the Hotel Beverly knows that there are extra people living there. The family doesn't have much money. Answers will vary. pp. 140–141*)

3. Why does Anita fill up the grocery cart? What does this say about her character? (*She wants to pretend her situation is carefree, like it was before the revolution when her family could pay for all the groceries they wanted. Answers will vary. pp. 147–148*)

4. Anita is not sure the United States is a free country for those who are not Americans. Do you think it is? Explain your answer. (*Answers will vary. p. 149*)

5. Anita knows when she sees Mr. Washburn at the apartment that her father is dead. Why does she deny it to herself until she hears the words? (*Answers will vary. pp. 150–151*)

6. **Prediction:** Will the family move to Queens to be with the Garcías?

Supplementary Activities

1. Research: Have students research how many immigrants come to the United States from the Dominican Republic. Students can consult census records.

2. Literary Elements: **Similes**—The nun's breath smells musty, "like an old suitcase that hasn't been opened in years" (p. 144). Have students write similes to describe other ways breath can smell.

3. Writing: Have students write a paragraph telling what Anita means when she says they are all "crying into the empty space at the center of our family" (p. 151).

4. Social Studies/Culture: Have students interview someone in the community who was born in a different country. Discuss whether or not it was hard to learn English and what was most difficult about adapting to America.

Chapter Eleven, pp. 152–163

Anita's family has moved in with the Garcías in Queens until they can find a nearby place. It's Thanksgiving Day, and the girls are outside waiting for the forecasted snow. They go in to eat dinner as the first flakes fall. Anita talks to Sam on the phone. He wants to visit New York and see the Yankees play. When Mr. Mancini came to New York, he brought a letter from Oscar. Anita wonders if she really loved Oscar. After dinner the girls go outside and make snow angels. That night, Anita looks down on the angels from a window, thinking that they resemble snow butterflies. In her mind, she promises Papi that she will fly free.

Vocabulary
accommodate (155)
lackluster (156)
sophisticated (156)
stressed (157)

Discussion Questions

1. Carla has adapted to living in America and acts like she's lived there a long time. How does Anita feel about this? *(Answers will vary. p. 152)*

2. Carla has a crush on a boy and explains to Anita that liking boys begins in seventh grade. Anita doesn't tell her that it happened to her in sixth grade. Why? *(Answers will vary. p. 153)*

3. There are many references to death in the novel. Mami mentions that trees look gray and dead. Tía Laura says the kids will catch deathly colds. Why does Anita feel that death isn't something to scare people with? Is this consistent with her character? Why? *(Her father has already experienced it, so it is no longer unknown to her. She believes it's more frightening to face living. Answers will vary. pp. 155, 162)*

4. How have Anita's feelings toward Oscar changed now that they are apart? *(She's uncertain how she feels about him because she feels so numb inside. p. 159)*

5. One of Anita's nightmares is that she's being buried alive. What could this nightmare represent? *(Answers will vary.)*

6. Anita thinks Chucha would say, "What good is it to escape captivity only to be imprisoned in your own misery?" Do you agree with her philosophy? *(Answers will vary. p. 162)*

7. Compare Anita's life to that of a butterfly. *(As a young child, Anita felt safe and secure at the compound, but as she grows older, she realizes that there is more to the world than what she has experienced. Her father wants her to break out of the coccoon she has lived in and experience freedom. He encourages her to fly away, and through moving to the United States where she is able to read, speak, and write freely, she will be able to do so.)*

8. How does the emptiness inside Anita finally begin to fill? *(She chooses to accept the gift her father sacrificed his life to give her: she chooses to embrace freedom and fly.)*

9. **Prediction:** Will Anita ever go back to live in the Dominican Republic?

Supplementary Activities

1. Literary Elements: **Similes**—Have students complete their list of similes. For example: the snow looks "like little tiny marshmallows" (p. 161)

2. Literary Analysis/Symbols: Have students complete their list of symbols. Mention the snow world that Anita sees as "a brand-new world no one's had the chance to ruin yet" (p. 161).

3. Writing: Have students pretend they are Anita and write a letter in response to Oscar.

4. Science: Have students contrast the climates of the Dominican Republic and New York City.

Post-reading Discussion Questions

1. With three adjectives, describe Anita as she was at the beginning of the novel. With three adjectives, describe her as she was at the end of the novel. Are your adjectives different? What do the different lists say about the changes in Anita?

2. The beginning of the novel describes Anita helping Carla. By the end of the novel, Carla is helping Anita. How has their relationship changed?

3. What have you learned about immigrants from this novel?

4. Papi sees Anita as being strong and brave. What do you think is the strongest and bravest thing she does?

5. What did you learn about dictatorships from this novel?

6. At an early point in the novel, Anita thinks she is free. When does she learn she is not free, and what change occurs in her at this time?

7. Why does Anita's opinion of Sammy change?

8. What do you think Oscar's life will be like in ten years?

9. Do you think the secret policemen have wives and children? Why or why not?

10. How does Anita's attitude toward Oscar change in the story?

11. What do you think of the García family escaping to the United States?

12. Julia Alvarez, author of *Before We Were Free*, wrote in her author's note, "It is the responsibility of those who survive the struggle for freedom to give testimony. To tell the story in order to keep alive the memory of those who died." Do you feel she wrote a balanced testimonial? Why or why not?

13. Why is the novel titled *Before We Were Free*?

14. Would you change the part in the novel when Papi is executed? Why or why not?

15. Why does Papi feel that education is the key to overcoming the problems in his country?

16. What have you learned about living without freedom?

17. Is it possible to find happiness, peace, and hope after enduring losses such as the ones Anita has had to endure in her young life?

18. Would you recommend this book to a friend? Why or why not?

Post-reading Extension Activities

1. Read aloud scenes in the novel with different students assuming different character roles.

2. Draw a picture of what your family compound would be like if you had one. Include homes for your extended family of aunts, uncles, and grandparents.

3. Find a recipe for *pastelitos*, make them, and share them with the class.

4. Julia Alvarez gets story ideas from her childhood and from historical events. Read a few pages from a recent history of the United States or a news magazine and make a list of potential story ideas.

5. Replot the story by having Pupo announce the liberation.

6. Explain how the book would have changed if Papi were not involved in the plot to overthrow the dictator.

7. Read reviews of Julia Alvarez's *Before We Were Free* on the Internet.

8. Visit Julia Alvarez's Web site at **www.alvarezjulia.com** and e-mail her your thoughts on the book.

9. Pick one chapter in the book and draw an illustration that could precede it.

10. Make a time line of the major events in the book with short annotations and illustrations.

Assessment for *Before We Were Free*

Assessment is an ongoing process. The following ten items can be completed during the novel study. Once finished, the student and teacher will check the work. Points may be added to indicate the level of understanding.

Name _____ Date _____

Student   **Teacher**

_____   _____   1. Keep a literary journal as you read the book.

_____   _____   2. Complete your Character Analysis chart and plot graph.

_____   _____   3. Give yourself credit for each vocabulary activity you complete.

_____   _____   4. Compare your list of symbols with those of your classmates. Prepare a chart of all the symbols and display it in your classroom.

_____   _____   5. Who is Anita? Create a collage of ideas and images significant to her.

_____   _____   6. Keep your writing about the book in a folder. Choose one of your best pieces to submit for evaluation.

_____   _____   7. Write an entry that Anita might write in her diary once she gets to the United States.

_____   _____   8. Write a letter to the librarian giving your evaluation of this book for classroom use.

_____   _____   9. Discuss the Post-reading Discussion Questions on page 26 of this guide with a partner. Write a multi-paragraph essay on one of them.

_____   _____   10. Choose one of the Post-reading Extension Activities to complete.